江苏概况

　　江苏地处中国大陆东部，是长三角的重要组成部分。全省国土面积 10.72 万平方公里，长江横贯东西，大运河穿境而过，水网密布，平原辽阔，历史上是著名的"鱼米之乡"。江苏现有 13 个设区市，下辖 96 个县（市、区），人口 8000 万，经济综合实力强，教育发达，文化繁荣，社会祥和，是"美丽中国"的生动缩影。

Overview

Situated in Eastern China, Jiangsu plays a vital role in the Yangtze Delta Region. With a land of 107,200 square kilometers, it is richly covered with water networks, in particular, the east-ward Yangtze River and the Beijing-Hangzhou Grand Canal. Added with a plain-dominated terrain, hence it is dubbed as 'a land of milk and honey'. Jiangsu Province covers 13 municipalities and 96 counties, with a population of 80 million. It's economy is strong, education advanced, culture booming and society harmonious— a vivid epitome of the beautiful China.

地形地貌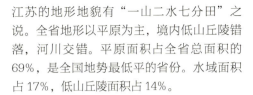

江苏的地形地貌有"一山二水七分田"之
说。全省地形以平原为主，境内低山丘陵错
落，河川交错。平原面积占全省总面积的
69%，是全国地势最低平的省份。水域面积
占17%，低山丘陵面积占14%。

江苏平原面积比例居全国各省首位，耕地面
积广阔。江苏是全国湿地资源最丰富的省份
之一，沿海滩涂占全国的1/4以上。

Terrain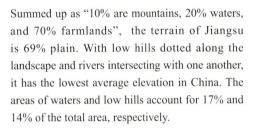

Summed up as "10% are mountains, 20% waters,
and 70% farmlands", the terrain of Jiangsu
is 69% plain. With low hills dotted along the
landscape and rivers intersecting with one another,
it has the lowest average elevation in China. The
areas of waters and low hills account for 17% and
14% of the total area, respectively.

Ranking No.1 in terms of ratio of plain to
provincial land mass, Jiangsu boasts a vast arable
area. Jiangsu is one of the most wetland-rich
provinces in China, and its coastal mudflat takes up
over 25% of the national total.

江苏境内有大小河流 2900 多条、大小湖泊 290 多个，中国五大淡水湖中的太湖、洪泽湖，分别镶嵌在江南水乡和苏北平原。

洪泽湖 Hongze Lake

太湖 Taihu Lake

Jiangsu is home to 2,900 rivers and 290 lakes of varied sizes. Taihu Lake and Hongze Lake, two of the top five freshwater lakes in China, are embedded in the south of the Yangtze River and the north of Jiangsu respectively.

长江 The Yangtze River

大运河　The Beijing-Hangzhou Grand Canal

淮河　The Huaihe River

江苏绝大部分地区在海拔50米以下，低山丘陵集中在西南和北部，主要有老山山脉、云台山脉、宁镇山脉、茅山山脉、宜溧山脉。

云台山脉——连云港花果山　Yuntai Mountains — Huaguoshan Mountain in Lian Yungang

The majority of Jiangsu's terrain is below the fifty-meter altitude line, and low hills and mountains concentrate at the southwest and the north, consisting of various mountains, like Laoshan Mountains, Yuntai Mountains, Ningzhen Mountains, Maoshan Mountains and Yili Mountains.

宁镇山脉——镇江茅山 Ningzhen Mountains — Maoshan Mountain in Zhenjiang

老山山脉 Laoshan Mountain

自然资源

自古有"苏湖熟，天下足"之美誉。江苏是我国重要的商品粮基地，粮食、棉花、油料等农作物遍布全省；水产资源十分丰富，盛产鱼类、虾类、蟹类、贝藻类水产品；多种矿产资源储量居全国前列。

Natural Resources

Quoting "the harvest of Jiangsu and Zhejiang satisfies whole China", Jiangsu is a producer of commodity grains, with grains, cotton, oil plants and other crops thriving across the land. It is rich in aquaculture products, especially fish, shrimps, crabs, shellfish and algae. Its mineral researves are among the top in China.

万亩油菜地　Rapeflower Field of thousands of acres

碧螺春茶　Biluochun Tea

水禽养殖 Waterfowl Farming

行政区划 ●

江苏得名于清朝江宁府和苏州府二府之首字，正式建制始于 1667 年，下辖南京、苏州、无锡、常州、镇江、扬州、泰州、南通、盐城、淮安、宿迁、徐州、连云港 13 个设区市。

南京市夜景 Nightscenes of Nanjing

Administrative Division

Jiangsu was officially established in 1667, with the name Jiang from "Jiangning" and Su from "Suzhou". It now has 13 cities, namely, Nanjing, Suzhou, Wuxi, Changzhou, Zhenjiang, Yangzhou, Taizhou, Nantong, Yancheng, Huai'an, Suqian, Xuzhou and Lian Yungang.

南京

江苏省省会城市，是中国四大古都之一，素有"六朝古都"、"十朝都会"之称。科教人才资源丰富，自古就有"天下文枢"之美誉。现拥有高校53所、两院院士80多位。南京山水城林融为一体，城市绿树掩映，曾荣获联合国人居奖特别荣誉奖、"国际花园城市"金奖等。

南京石象路 Shixiang Road of Nanjing

Nanjing

Nanjing, capital of Jiangsu, is one of the Four Great Ancient Capitals of China, with a reputation of "Capital of Six Dynasties and Ten Regimes". With advanced education and rich talents, it has long been known as the "Center of Culture Under Heaven". It now houses 53 colleges and universities and over 80 academecians of Chinese Academy of Chinese Academy of Sciences and Chinese Academy of Engineering. Owning a well-integrated environment of hills, waters, towns and lush trees, Nanjing has won the special honor of UN Habitat Scroll of Honor Award and the golden award of International Garden City.

南京美龄宫 Nanjing Soong Mei-ling Palace

南京夫子庙　Nanjing Confucious Temple

苏州

素有"人间天堂"之美誉。以"小桥流水、粉墙黛瓦、史迹名园"为独特风貌，是全国著名的历史文化名城和风景旅游城市。苏州历代英才辈出，名人灿若群星，是吴文化的发祥地。经济发达，地区生产总值位居全国所有城市第7位，是国家高新技术产业基地。

Suzhou

Suzhou has long been known as "Paradise on Earth". With bridges over streams, black tiles over white walls and numerous relics and gardens, it is well-known as a historical and cultural city as well as a tourism city and tourism city. As a cradle of Wu culture, Suzhou gave birth to myriads of prominent figures throughout Chinese history. With GDP ranking No.7 in China, it is economically competitive and positioned as a national cluster of high-tech companies.

苏州市全景　Panorama of Suzhou

苏州盘门　Panmen Gate in Suzhou

苏州人家 Suzhou Households

无锡市全景 Panorama of Wuxi

无锡

历史悠久、人文荟萃，有 3000 余年历史。经济发达，是中国民族工商业和乡镇企业的摇篮，素有"布码头"、"丝市"、"米市"之称。无锡被誉为"太湖明珠"，有"江南之美在太湖，太湖之美在无锡"一说，是国家环保模范城市、中国优秀旅游城市。

Wuxi

Built three thousand years ago, Wuxi has a rich cultural heritage. With well-developed economy, it is the cradle of Chinese national industry and township businesses, boasting a reputation of "Cloth Pier", "Silk Market" and "Rice Market". Dubbed "Pearl of Taihu Lake", Wuxi is described in the quote "the beauty of South Jiangsu lies in Taihu Lake, whereas the beauty of the southern Yangtze River". It is a paradigm city for ecological conservation and tourism.

无锡蠡园　Liyuan Garden in Wuxi

无锡清名桥 Qingming Bridge in Wuxi

常州

别称"龙城"，位于江苏南部，与上海、南京等距相望。常州制造业实力强，是现代装备制造名城，轨道交通装备、光伏、石墨烯等产业加速发展；职业教育发达，被誉为"银领摇篮"；旅游资源丰富，是中国著名的旅游文化名城。

常州市全景　Panorama of Changzhou

Changzhou

Changzhou, also known as the Dragon Town, sits at the south of Jiangsu and is in equal distance to Shanghai and Nanjing. It is a manufacturing powerhouse in modern equipment, with railway equipment, photovoltaic and graphene industries growing fast. As its vocational education leads China, it is known as the "cradle of silver-collars". Its tourism resources are abundant, hence being known as a famous tourism and cultural city in China.

常州外城河 The Outer City Canal of Changzhou

常州天宁寺 Changzhou Tianning Temple

镇江

古称"润州"，历史上有"南北要津"、"九省通衢"之称，长江和京杭大运河在此交汇。镇江历史文化底蕴深厚、人文荟萃，市内有金山寺、西津渡等众多名胜古迹，有"天下第一江山"之美誉。

镇江市全景 Panorama of Zhenjiang

Zhenjiang

Zhenjiang, previously called Runzhou, was a citadel linking the South to the North and a transportation center for nine provinces in Chinese history. It is where the Yangtze River and the Grand Canal meet. Zhenjiang is imbued with a rich cultural and historical heritage and numerous places of interest including Jinshan Temple and Xijin Ferry, hence winning the title "Best Landscape on Earth".

镇江西津古渡 *Zhenjiang Xijin Ferry*

镇江北固楼 Beigu Pavilion in Zhenjiang

镇江焦山 Jiangshan Mountain in Zhenjiang

扬州市全景 Panorama of Yangzhou

扬州

扬州曾经是中国古代最繁华的商业城市，历史悠久，文化昌盛，有"淮左名都，竹西佳处"之称。以"扬州八怪"为代表的扬州画派和扬州学派，在中国历史上影响深远。扬州是人文名城，曾荣获"联合国人居奖"。

扬州文昌阁　Wenchang Pavillion in Yangzhou

扬州东关街 Dongguan Street in Yangzhou

Yangzhou

Dubbed "Regional Capital of Huainandao and Beauty in Zhuxi" (ancient name of Yangzhou), Yangzhou was once the most prosperous center of business in China with rich culture. Yangzhou Painting School and Yangzhou Literary School represented by Eight Eccentrics of Yangzhou have a profound impact on Chinese history. As a culture-friendly city, Yangzhou has won UN-Habitat Scroll Award.

扬州瘦西湖 Slender West Lake in Yangzhou

泰州市全景　Panorama of Taizhou

泰州

位于江苏中部、长江北岸，是承南启北的水陆要津。泰州生态好、环境美，垛田和水上森林闻名遐迩，是一座宜居宜养的康泰之州。

Taizhou

Taizhou, lying at the northern bank of the Yangtze River and the heart of Jiangsu, is a water and land logistics hub linking the south and the north. With sound ecology and beautiful environment, Taizhou is known for the stacking farmland and forest lake, making it a livable land conducive to people's health.

泰州药王塔　Yaowang Pagoda in Taizhou

南通

被誉为"中国近代第一城"。南通滨江临海，
集"黄金海岸"与"黄金水道"优势于一身，
是中国首批对外开放的 14 个沿海城市之一；
是著名的"纺织之乡"、"体育之乡"、"教
育之乡"、"建筑之乡"、"长寿之乡"。

南通市全景　Panorama of Nantong

Nantong

Nantong is dubbed the "First Urban City in Comtemporary China". Adjecent to both rivers and the sea, Nantong shows advantages in having the Gold Coast and Gold Waterway and is one of the first fourteen coastal cities opening to the world. A land known for textiles, sports, education, construction and longevity.

南通狼山　Langshan Mountain in Nantong

盐城

因"环城皆盐场"得名，是淮剧发源地和"中国杂技之乡"。拥有江苏省最长的海岸线、最大的沿海滩涂、最广的海域面积，建有麋鹿和丹顶鹤两个国家级自然保护区。

Yancheng

Yancheng, a city of salt fields, is the cradle of Huai Opera and Chinese acrobatics. Endowed with the longest coastal line, the largest mudflat and the broadest sea area in China, it has also established national natural reserves for milu deers and red-crowned cranes.

盐城市全景　Panorama of Yancheng

盐城麋鹿自然保护区　*Milu Deer Nature Reserve in Yancheng*

淮安市全景　Panorama of Huai'an

淮安

位于中国南北地理分割线上，境内有中国第四大淡水湖——洪泽湖。淮安历史悠久，有著名的青莲岗文化遗址，历史上曾是漕运枢纽、盐运要冲。

Huai'an

Sitting at the geographical divide between southern and northern China, Huai'an owns Hongze Lake, one of the Four Great Freshwater Lakes in China. Boasting a long history, Huai'an holds a former site of Qingliangang Culture and once was a hub for river logistics and salt transport.

淮安里运河　The Huai'an Li Canal

宿迁

江苏省最年轻的设区市。洪泽湖和骆马湖南北相望，大运河和古黄河纵贯东西，是中国唯一一个拥有两湖两河的设区市。有"中国白酒之都"的称号，也是中国著名的"花卉之乡"、"杨树之乡"。

Suqian

As the most recent established city in Jiangsu, Suqian is the only Chinese city that is amidst two lakes and two rivers, namely, Hongze Lake and Luoma Lake at the north and south, the Grand Canal and the Yellow River across the east and west. Known for producing Chinese liquor, Suqian is called a "land of flowers and poplars".

宿迁市全景 Panorama of Suqian

宿迁七彩衲田　Seven-colored Patched Fields in Suqian

徐州市全景 Panorama of Xuzhou

徐州

古称彭城，地处苏鲁豫皖四省交界处，是江苏的"北大门"。历史上为华夏九州之一，是两汉文化的发源地。徐州是全国综合交通枢纽城市，素有"五省通衢"之称。徐州是淮海经济区中心城市，有"中国工程机械之都"的美誉。

Xuzhou

Formerly named Pengcheng, Xuzhou is at the juncture of four provinces — Jiangsu, Shandong, Henan and An'hui, making it Jiangsu's gate to the north. It once was one of the Nine Ancient States and the cradle of the West Han culture. Xuzhou offers holistic transportation connecting five provinces. As a core city in the Huaihai Economic Zone, Xuzhou is titled China's Capital of Engineering Machinery.

徐州汉文化景区　Han Cultural Scenic Area in Xuzhou

连云港

全国首批沿海开放城市。连云港港是中国主枢纽港、集装箱干线港，亚欧大陆桥起点，中亚出海通道。连云港文化旅游资源丰富，花果山是中国古典四大名著《西游记》的取材地。

Lian Yungang

Lian Yungang is one of the first coastal cities opening to the world, the starting point of Eurasian Continental Bridge and the sea passage to Central Asia. Lian Yungang Port is a major container port in China. It is a city with numerous attractions, especially Huaguo Mountain, which gave inspirations to Journey to the West, one of the Four Famous Classics of China.

连云港苏马湾　Suma Bay in Lian Yungang

连云港市全景　*Panorama of Lian Yungang*

历史文化

　　江苏是中华文明的重要发祥地之一，历史悠久，文化源远流长。千百年来，孕育了吴文化、楚汉文化、金陵文化、淮扬文化，形成了南秀北雄的鲜明地域文化。全省现有 13 座历史文化名城，数量占全国的 1/10，名胜古迹星罗棋布，江南园林、水乡古镇声名远播，昆曲、古琴、云锦、苏绣等各类文化遗珍不胜枚举。

History and Culture

Jiangsu is an important birthplace of the Chinese Civilization, with a profound historical and cultural heritage. Over the course of several millennia, it has fostered Wu Culture, Chu and Han Culture, Jinling Culture and Huaiyang Culture, adding elegance to South China, in comparison to the North being pridominantly masculine. Jiangsu contains thirteen Historical and Cultural Towns, taking up 10% nationwide. Places of interest and historical relics are spotted across the land. Gardens and water towns are favored by both Chinese and non-Chinese alike. Cultural heritages such as Kunqu Opera, Guqin Zither, Cloud Brocade and Suzhou Embroidery are countless.

文化溯源

南京汤山溶洞留下的"南京猿人化石",让江苏的人类文明史追溯到 30 多万年之前。以青莲岗文化、良渚文化为代表的新石器时代文化遗址在江苏境内分布众多。

青莲岗文化是新石器文化的一个分支,年代约为公元前 5400—前 4400 年。

A branch of Neolithic Culture, Qingliangang Culture existed around 5,400-4,400 BC.

散落在江浙一带的良渚文化被称为"中华文明之光",是中华文明的重要源头之一。

Regarded as the "Beam of the Chinese Civilization", Liangzhu Culture is found in areas of Jiangsu and Zhejiang.

Origin of Culture

Nanjing Ape Fossils discoverd in Tanshang Carst Cave in Nanjing bring Jiangsu's human civilization back to as early as 300,000 years ago. Neolithic sites represented by Qingliangang Culture and Liangzhu Culture are widely discovered in Jiangsu.

汉画像 Bas-Relief Images of the Han Dynasty

徐州汉兵马俑陪葬坑　Funerary Pit with Han Terra Cotta Warriors in Xuzhou

徐州是两汉文化的集萃之地，故人称"秦唐看西安，明清看北京，两汉看徐州"。徐州的汉墓、汉兵马俑、汉画像石并称为"汉代三绝"。

Recognized by a saying " Qin and Tang culture in Xi'an, Ming and Qing culture in Beijing and East and West Han culture in Xuzhou", Xuzhou gathers the essence of East and West Han cultures. Han Tombs, Han Terra-Cotta Warriors and Han Painting are collectively known as the Three Impeccable Feats.

历史文化名城

江苏是全国拥有历史文化名城最多的省份，有南京、苏州、扬州、徐州、镇江、淮安、无锡、南通、泰州、常州、常熟、宜兴、高邮，共13个。

Famous Historical and Cutural Cities

Jiangsu possesses thirteen (the largest number in China) historically and culturally famous cities and towns, namely, Nanjing, Suzhou, Yangzhou, Xuzhou, Zhenjiang, Huai'an, Wuxi, Nantong, Taizhou, Changzhou, Changshu, Yixing and Gaoyou.

常熟市全景 Panorama of Changshu

Changshu

People in Changshu build their houses near rivers, forming a scene of small bridges over water and deep alleys in tranquility, a custom that is observed since the Ming and Qing Dynasty. Great artists in literature, calligraphy, book collection, zither playing, and painting have emerged here since the Tang Dynasty.

常熟

民居枕河而筑，小桥流水人家，街巷幽深静谧，至今仍保持明清时的格局。自唐以来，在文化、书法、藏书、古琴、绘画等领域名人辈出。

常熟市虞山尚湖　Lake Shang in Yushan Township, Changshu

宜兴

设县于秦始皇时期，是中国最早的县之一。保留了明清以来150多座形态不一的古桥梁。盛产紫砂壶，是中国著名的"陶都"。

Yixing

Built during Emperor Yingzheng's rein of the Qin Dynasty, Yixing is one of the oldest counties in China. 150 bridges built around the Ming and Qing Dynasty have been preserved. Yixing is also known as potter town in China for its production of purple clay pots.

宜兴市全景 Panorama of Yixing

Gaoyou

With ancient tiltles of Famous District to the East of the Yangtze River and Top County in Guangling, Gaoyou was named after a tall tower (hence the name "Gao") built by Emperor Yingzheng in 223 BC and a post house (hence the name "you") during the same period — the only city amongst 2,000 plus cities and towns with "you" in the name. The ancient architectural style is well-preserved with a salient feature of postal cultures.

高邮

史称"江左名区"、"广陵首邑"，秦王嬴政于公元前 223 年在此筑高台、置邮亭，故名高邮，是中国 2000 多个县市中唯一以邮命名的城市。古城传统格局和风貌保存完好，邮驿文化特色突出。

高邮市盂城驿　Yucheng Post House in Gaoyou

苏州市周庄镇 Zhouzhuang Township, Suzhou

淮安市河下镇　Hexia Township, Huai'an

徐州市窑湾镇　Yaowan Township, Xuzhou

南京市桠溪镇 Yaxi Township, Nanjing

苏州市甪直镇　Luzhi Township, Suzhou

苏州市千灯镇　Qiandeng Township, Suzhou

文学书画 ●

中国四大古典名著《红楼梦》《西游记》《水浒传》《三国演义》享誉世界，均出自江苏籍作者之手或与江苏有关。以"吴门画派"、"金陵画派"、"扬州八怪"为代表的江苏书画艺术，在中国画坛享有盛名。

四大名著　The Four Famous Classics of China

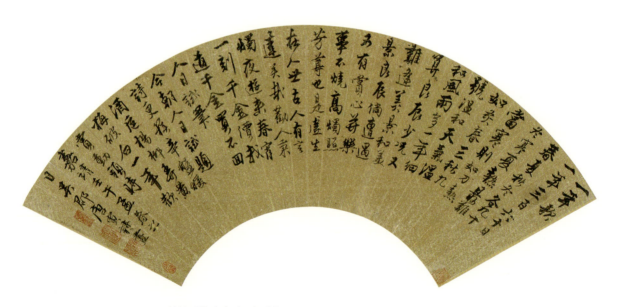

吴门画派 唐寅《一年歌》　*One Year Song* by Tang Yin, Wumen Painting School

Literature and Painting ●

The Four Famous Ancient Classics, namely, Dream of the Red Chamber, Journey to the West, All Men and Brothers and Three Kingdom are either written by authors with a Jiangsu pedigree or are relevant to Jiangsu. Jiangsu paintings represented by Wumen Painting School, Jinling Painting School and Yangzhou Eight Accentrics are highly appreciated in Chinese circle of painting.

吴门画派 文徵明 《五月江深图》
May River in Tranquility by Wen Zhengming, Wumen Painting School

金陵画派 龚贤 《水墨山水图》
Landscape Painitng by Gong Xian, Jinling Painting School

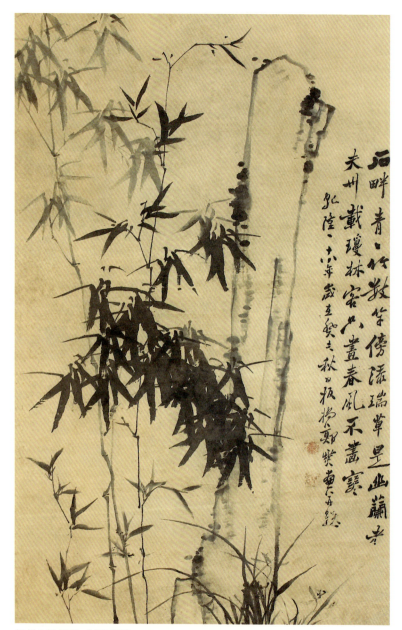

石畔青々竹数竿 傍添瑞草更幽蘭
夫州戴瓊林容氏畫春風不盡寒
乾隆六年歲立癸之秋日板橋鄭燮畫寒蘭九絲

扬州八怪 郑燮 《竹石图》 *Bamboo and Stone* by Zheng Xie, Yangzhou Eight Accentrics

扬州八怪 罗聘《梅花图卷》 *Scroll of Plum Flowers* by Luo Pin, Yangzhou Eight Accentrics

新金陵画派 徐悲鸿《八骏图》 *A Portrait of Eight Breed* by Xu Beihong, Neo-jinling Paiting School

戏曲曲艺 ●———————

江苏有 20 多个各具特色的地方戏剧。"百戏之祖"昆曲发源于江苏，京剧大师梅兰芳出生于此。还有锡剧、扬剧、评弹、淮剧、柳琴梆子、白局等众多的曲艺种类。

昆曲《桃花扇》 Kunqu Opera *The Peach Blossom*

昆曲《牡丹亭》 Kunqu Opera *Peony Pavillion*

京剧《贵妃醉酒》 Peking Opera *The Drunken Beauty*

京剧大师梅兰芳（1894–1961）
Mei Lanfang — Master of Peking Opera

Operas

Jiangsu has over twenty local operas with distinctive features. Kunqu Opera, father of hundreds of operas, originated in Jiangsu, and Mei Lanfang, master of Peking Opera, was born here. There are also Wuxi Opera, Yangzhou Opera, Pingtan, Huai Opera, Liuqin Bangzi and Baiju.

1 锡剧《庵堂认母》 ————————

锡剧发端于古老的吴歌，是江苏苏南一带说唱艺术的一大分支。

2 淮剧《莲花庵》 ————————

淮剧发源于清代的盐城，活跃于淮安、泰州一带。

3 扬剧《百岁挂帅》 ————————

扬剧兴起于江苏扬州，主要流行扬州、镇江、泰州一带。

4 苏州评弹 ————————

评弹以说表细腻见长，吴侬软语娓娓动听，活跃于苏州一带。

1	2	3
	4	

Wuxi Opera
Birth Mother in Buddhist Nunnery

Originated from songs of the Wu Kingdom, Wuxi Opera is one main branch of South Jiangsu folk musicals.

Yangzhou Opera
The Centenarian Commander

Yangzhou Opera originated in Yangzhou and became popular in Yangzhou, Zhenjiang and Taizhou.

Huai Opera
Lotus Nunnery

Huai Opera emerged from Yancheng in the Qing Dynasty and became popular in Huai'an and Taizhou.

Suzhou Pingtan

Pingtan is featured with soft tones in Suzhou dialect and is widely accepted in Suzhou.

非物质文化遗产 ●————

在灿若星河的中国非物质文化遗产中，江苏瑰宝璀璨夺目。云锦、苏绣、雕版印刷、古琴等各种传统工艺巧夺天工。

Intangible Cultural Heritages ●——

Amid the galaxy of Chinese intangible cultural heritages, the ones from Jiangsu are the brightest stars. Cloud Brocade, Suzhou Embroidery, Woodblock Printing and Guqin Zither are unmatched crafts.

剪纸 Paper Cutting

云锦织造　Weaving Cloud Brocades

雕版印刷 Woodblock Printing

古琴 Guqin Zither

古典园林 ●

江南园林是中国古典园林的杰出代表，凝聚了
江南能工巧匠的勤劳和智慧，蕴涵了中国传统
哲学、宗教思想及山水诗、画等传统艺术，自
古以来就吸引着无数中外游人。

苏州拙政园 Zhuozhengyuan Garden in Suzhou

苏州留园　Liuyuan Garden in Suzhou

Classic Gardens

Gardens in South Jiangsu are representatives among Chinese Classic Gardens, which encapsulate the diligence and wisdom of artisans in the region and integrate Chinese traditional philosophy, religious thinking and scenic poems and paintings.

"江南园林甲天下，苏州园林甲江南。"中
国四大名园中的拙政园、留园都是世界文化
遗产苏州园林的代表。留园内的冠云峰体现
了太湖石"瘦、皱、漏、透"的精髓。

苏州沧浪亭 Canglangting Pavilion in Suzhou

苏州网师园　Wangshiyuan Garden in Suzhou

Quoting "gardens in the south of Yangtze River are the best in China while the Suzhou gardens are the best among them", Humble Adminstrator Garden and Lingering Garden, two of the Four Great Gardens in China are representatives of Suzhou Gardens, which are the world cultural heritages. Guanyun Peak in Lingering Garden contains the essential features of "lean, wrinkle, leaky and lucid" stones from Taihu Lake.

扬州何园 Heyuan Garden in Yangzhou

扬州园林以舒朗为鲜明特色，院落组合、水景处理、山石安排独具风格。

With salient features of being open and clear, Yangzhou Gardens are unique in room arrangment, pond layout and bonsai organization.

扬州个园 Geyuan Garden in Yangzhou

南京瞻园布局典雅精致，已有 600 多年的历史。

Zhanyuan Garden in Nanjing was built 600 years ago with a classic and exquisite layout.

南京瞻园 Zhanyuan Garden in Nanjing

Jichang Garden is famous for the natural appearance of rockery, exquisite ponds, condense arrangement, crudity of trees and briliant design of sceneries.

无锡寄畅园，成名于其山的自然、水的精美、园的凝练、树的古拙和景的巧妙。

无锡寄畅园 *Jichangyuan Garden in Wuxi*

寻味美食

江苏菜肴大致可分为淮扬、京苏、苏锡、徐海四种风味。"淮扬菜系"为我国四大著名菜系之一,影响最广,常被当作江苏菜的代称。

Seeking Delicacies

Jiangsu cuisine can be largely divided into four branches — Huaiyang, Jingsu, Suxi and Xuhai. Huaiyang cuisine is one of the Four Famous cuisine in China with a far-reaching impact and it is a beacon of Jiangsu dishes.

狮子头 Large Meatball

大煮干丝 Stewed Dried Toufu

淮安软兜 Huai'an Stewed Eel

文思豆腐 Wensi Toufu Slices

太湖三白——白虾　Three White Delicacies of Taihu Lake (White shrimps)

太湖三白——白鱼　Three White Delicacies of Taihu Lake (White fish

在江苏的众多美食中，"长江三鲜"（鲥鱼、
刀鱼、河豚）和"太湖三白"（白鱼、银鱼、
白虾）以其口味鲜美、营养丰富而名扬天下。

Three Delicacies of the Yangtze River—shad,
swordfish and pufferfish, and Three White
Delicacies of Taihu Lake—whitefish, silver fish
and white shrimps are known both home and
abroad for the fresh and savoury tastes and rich
nutrition.

太湖三白——银鱼　Three White Delicacies of Taihu Lake (Silver fish)

江鲜河豚　Pufferfish

扬州蟹黄包　Yangzhou Crab-Roe Buns

宗教文化 ●────────

江苏有佛教、道教、伊斯兰教、天主教、基督教五大宗教。

佛教——南京牛首山佛顶寺　Buddhism — Usnisa Temple in Niushou Mountain, Nanjing

Religions

Buddhism, Taoism, Islamism, Catholicism and Christianity are the five main religions in Jiangsu.

佛教——苏州寒山寺 Buddhism — Hanshan Temple in Suzhou

佛教——扬州大明寺 Buddhism — Daming Temple in Yangzhou

佛教——南京栖霞寺　Buddhism — Qixia Temple in Nanjing

佛教——无锡灵山大佛 Buddhism — Lingshan Grand Buddha in Wuxi

道教——镇江茅山乾元观　Taoism — Maoshan Qianyuan Palace in Zhenjiang

伊斯兰教——扬州仙鹤寺　Islamism — Crane Temple in Yangzhou

天主教——无锡三里桥天主堂 Catholicism — Sanliqiao Church in Wuxi

基督教——南京圣保罗堂 Christianity — Nanjing St. Paul's Church

经济活力

　　江苏是中国经济发展最具活力的地区之一。上世纪80年代，率先创办乡镇企业，实现由农到工转变；90年代，大力发展开放型经济，实现由内到外转变；进入新世纪，加快发展创新型经济，正在实现由大到强转变。2016年全省地区生产总值达7.6万亿元人民币，占全国的1/10以上。拥有全国最大的制造业集群，产业结构实现了"三二一"的历史性转变。现在，正着力推进扬子江城市群和沿海经济带、江淮生态经济区、淮海经济区中心城市"1+3"重点功能区格局，进一步优化江苏经济地理版图。

Economic Power

Jiangsu is one of the most economically dynamic regions in China. In the 1980s, Jiangsu took the lead in setting up township businesses and shifted from agriculture to industry. In the 1990s, Jiangsu vigorously developed open economy, turning the economy from inward to outward. Since entering the 21st Century, Jiangsu expedited the development of innovation-driven economy, changing from quantitiy to quality. As of 2016, provincial GDP stood at 7.6 trillion yuan, accounting for over 10% of the national total. Having the largest manufacturing cluster in China, it is on a unprecedented course of rearranging the output volume ranking service first, manufacturing second and agriculture third. Now, it exerts full efforts on promoting a 1+3 structure consisting of the Yangtze River City Cluster and major cities in the Coastal Economic Belt, the Jianghuai Ecological Ecomonic Zone and the Huaihai Economic Zone, optimizing its economic landscape.

现代农业 ●

江苏是全国 13 个粮食主产省之一，农业综合生产能力持续提升，现代农业发展步伐加快，家庭农场、合作社、种田大户等新业态、新模式蓬勃发展。

东辛农场 Dongxin Farmland

大沙河红富士苹果 Dashahe Fuji Apple

Mondern Agriculture ●

As one of the thirteen major grain producers in China, Jiangsu continues to bolster comprehensive agro-productivity and accelerate the development of modern agriculture, with new models and forms emerging such as family farmland, agricultural cooperatives and farmers with large-scale land.

阳山水蜜桃 Yangshan Peach

垛田油菜　Rapeflower at Stacking Fields

先进制造业 ●

江苏是中国重要的制造业基地。2016年，规模以上工业销售总额超过 16 万亿元。工业门类齐全，有冶金、化工、机械、纺织、医药、建材、轻工、电子八大支柱产业。百亿工业企业达到120 家。

Advanced Manufacturing ●

Jiangsu is a manufacturing powerhouse in China. As of 2016, total sales volume of all above-scale industries exceeded 16 trillion yuan. Jiangsu has comprehensive industrial categorization, with eight pillar industries of metallurgy, chemicals, machinery, textiles, pharmaceuticals, construction materials, light industry and electronics. The number of businesses with output exceeding ten billion yuan hit 120.

冶金、化工、机械、纺织、轻工、电子信息六大产业产值超万亿。

Metallurgy, chemicals, machinery, textiles, light industry and digital information all achieved one triliion yuan or more.

徐工集团（机械） XCMG (Machinery)

扬子石化－巴斯夫有限公司（化工） BASF-YPC Company Limited (Chemical)

沙钢集团（冶金） Shagang Group (Metallurgy)

海澜之家（纺织） HLA (Textile)

台湾积体电路制造股份有限公司（电子信息） TSMC (Digital Information)

镇江恒顺集团（轻工） Hengshun Group (Light Industry)

战略性新兴产业发展迅猛，有力促进了江苏经济转型升级和发展方式转变，产值占规模以上工业比重超过30%。南京未来网络、常州石墨烯、苏州纳米、无锡物联网、泰州生物医药等战略性新兴产业快速崛起。全社会研发投入占地区生产总值的比重达2.61%，科技进步贡献率达到61%。

常州石墨烯产业园，是正在崛起的"东方碳谷"
Changzhou Graphene Industrial Park, an Emerging Carbon Valley in the Orient

Strategic emerging industries are growing with a strong momentum, which boosted the transformation and upgrading of the economic structure and development models. The output of these industries take up over 30% of that of all above-scale industries in Jiangsu. Future internet in Nanjing, graphene in Changzhou, nanotechnology in Suzhou, IOT in Wuxi and bio-medicine in Taizhou and other emerging industries have all been rising fast. Investment on R&D took up 2.61% of GDP, and Jiangsu contributed 61% to technology advancement nationwide.

协鑫集团拥有中国最大的光伏电站
GCL Group Owns China's Largest Photovoltaic Power Station

世界智能制造大会　World Intelligent Manufacturing Summit

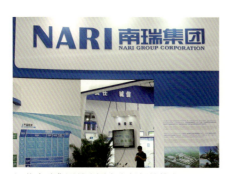

江苏南瑞集团是中国十大创新软件企业之一
Jiangsu NARI Group is one of China's Top 10 Innovative Software Business

泰州医药城是中国第一家国家级医药高新区
China Medical City in Taizhou is China's First National High-Tech Zone for Medicine

龙源电力集团海上风力发电　Offshore Wind Powerstation of Longyuan Power Group

现代服务业 ●

江苏大力发展服务业，2016年全省服务业增加值占GDP比重达50.1%。研发设计、物流仓储、现代金融、文化创意、商业服务等现代服务业已占到全省服务业的"半壁江山"。

Modern Service Industry ●

Jiangsu is vigorously developing the service sector. In 2016, added value of service industry took up 50.1% of total GDP. R&D design, logistics and warehousing, modern finance, creative industry, business services already took up half of the whole service sector in Jiangsu.

南京河西金融中心　Hexi Financial Center in Nanjing

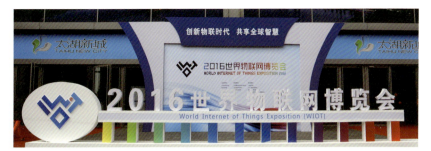

物联网产业蓬勃兴起　Booming IOT Industries

京东宿迁产业园　Jingdong Industrial Park in Suqian

惠龙易通物流控制中心　Logistics Control Center of Wellong Etown

县域经济 ●———————

江苏县域经济发达，2017年7月13日，工信部发布了《2017年中国县域经济百强县白皮书》，百强县中江苏占22席，其中前四名均来自江苏。

County Economy ●———————

County economy in Jiangsu is rather vigorous. On July 13, 2017, Ministry of Industry and Information Technology issued a whitepaper on Top 100 County Economies in 2017, where 22 are from Jiangsu with the top four seats occupied all by Jiangsu counties.

2017年中国县域经济综合竞争力百强排行榜前十强
Top 10 in 2017 China Top 100 Counties by Comprehensive Economic Strength

1	江苏昆山市	Kunshan Jiangsu Province
2	江苏江阴市	Jiangyin Jiangsu Province
3	江苏张家港市	Zhang Jiagang Jiangsu Province
4	江苏常熟市	Changshu Jiangsu Province

苏州昆山是全国首个 GDP 超过 3000 亿元的县级市，是"台资高地"。

China's first county-level city to achieve a GDP larger than 300 billion yuan, Kunshan, a county-level city in Suzhou, is the "gravity center" of capital from Taiwan.

昆山在 2017 年中国县域经济百强榜中排名第一
Kunshan was Ranked No.1 in 2017 Among the Top 100 Counties in China

无锡江阴是全国上市企业数量最多的县级市，被誉为"中国资本第一县"，有上市公司44家。

Dubbed No.1 County for IPO in China, Jiangyin in Wuxi has 44 listed companies, the largest number among all counties in China.

中国资本第一县——江阴
Jiangyin — China's No.1 County for IPO

张家港不仅是经济强市，社会精神文明建设也走在全国前列，连续多次荣膺"全国文明城市"称号。

Competitive in economy, Zhang Jiagang is a leader in civility building, winning the award of "national civilized city" consecutive times.

全国第一个县级文明城市——张家港

Zhang Jiagang — the First County-Level Civilized City in China

交通设施

　　江苏现代交通网络体系基本形成。沿江沿海港口连接五洲四海，内河航运里程约 24000 公里，居全国第一。全省高速公路通车里程 4660 公里。干线铁路建成里程 2791 公里，京沪高铁、沪宁城际高铁、宁杭高铁构成江苏高铁交通"铁三角"。拥有 9 个民用机场，开通直飞东南亚、北美、欧洲、澳洲等多条航线。

Transportation Connectivity

Modern transportation network is basically in shape. River and sea ports link Jiangsu with the whole world, with a inland water navigation mileage of about 24,000 kilometers, ranking No.1 in China. Mileage of highway across Jiangsu registers at 4,660 kilometers. Railway mileage has reached 2,791 kilometers, with Beijing-Shanghai Highspeed Railway, Shanghai-Nanjing Inner-city Highspeed Railway and Nanjing-Hangzhou HighSpeed Railway forming a high-speed triangle. Jiangsu houses nine civil airports, with non-stop flights to Southeast Asia, North America, Europe and Australia.

水上运输 ●

江苏现有万吨级泊位480个，是全国万吨级泊位最多的省份。
连云港港、南京港、太仓港是江苏最重要的集装箱干线港，
货运吞吐量合计67312万吨。

连云港港 Lian Yungang Port

Water Transportation

Jiangsu now owns 480 10,000 dwt berths—the largest number among all provinces. Lian Yungang Port, Nanjing Port and Taicang Port are the most critical container ports in Jiangsu, with a total cargo throughput reaching 67.312 billion tons.

江苏桥梁 ●——————

江苏桥梁的数量和建造技术都走在中国前列，
拥有 10 座跨江大桥、一座跨海大桥。

南京长江大桥 1968 年 12 月通车
Nanjing Yangtze River Bridge was Opened to Traffic in December 1968

润扬大桥 2005 年 10 月通车
Run-Yang Bridge was Opened to Traffic in October 2005

苏通大桥 2008 年 6 月通车
苏通大桥是全球首座超千米跨径斜拉桥
Suzhou-Nantong Bridge was Opened to Traffic in June 2008
Suzhou-Nantong Bridge is the World's First Long Span Cable-Stayed Bridge over One Thousand Meters

Bridges in Jiangsu

Jiangsu leads China in terms of bridge numbers and techniques of bridge building, with ten river-crossing bridges and one sea-crossing bridge.

连云港田湾跨海大桥 2016 年 4 月通车
Tianwan Sea-Crossing Bridge in Lian Yungang was Opened to Traffic in April 2016

昆山中环立交
Middle Ring Overpass in Kunshan

高速路网

江苏高速路网建设走在全国前列，密度达到 4.54 公里／百平方公里。

Highway Network

Jiangsu stays ahead of the curve in building highway networks, reaching a density of 4.54 kilometers per 100 square kilometers.

高速铁路

江苏正在建设设区市及周边大中城市"1.5 小时交通圈"。

Highspeed Railway

Jiangsu is building a 1.5 hour commuting circle linking cities within and surrounding the province.

南京南站
Nanjing South Railway Station

高速铁路
High-Speed Railway

南京禄口机场
Lukou Airport in Nanjing

机场航运 ●

从江苏起飞的数百条航线，构成了江苏对外往来的空中通道。
2016 年江苏民航客货吞吐能力为 3725.7 万人次和 51.6 万吨，
其中国际航线旅客吞吐量为 238.3 万人次。

Aviation

Several hundred flights take off from Jiangsu, forming an air passage between Jiangsu and the world. In 2016, civil airplanes in Jiangsu carried 37.257 million passengers and 516 thousands of tons goods. International flights from Jiangsu carried 2.383 million passengers.

连云港
白塔埠机场
Lian Yungang
Baitabu
Airport

连云港市
Lian Yungang

徐州市
Xuzhou

徐州
观音机场
Xuzhou
Guanyin Airport

宿迁市
Suqian

淮安市
Hual'an

盐城市
Yancheng

盐城
南洋机场
Yancheng
Nanyang
Airport

东京
Tokyo

淮安
涟水机场
Huai'an
Lianshui
Airport

泰州市
Taizhou

温哥华
Vancouver

扬泰机场
Yangzhou Taizhou
Airport

扬州市
Yangzhou

南通市
Nantong

南通
东兴机场
Nantong
Dongxing
Airport

仁川
Inchon

法兰克福
Frankfurt

南京
禄口机场
Nanjing
Lukou Airport

镇江市
Zhenjiang

南京市
Nanjing

常州市
Changzhou

无锡市
Wuxi

苏州市
Suzhou

洛杉矶
Los Angeles

常州
奔牛机场
Changzhou
Benniu Airport

悉尼
Sydney

甲米
Krabi

苏南
硕放机场
Southern Jiangsu
Shuofang
Airport

教育科技

　　"天下才子，半出江南。"江苏历来崇文重教、人才辈出。现有中国科学院院士 43 名、中国工程院院士 54 名，高等院校 167 所，在校大学生超过 190 万人。区域创新能力连续 8 年全国第一，全省发明专利申请和授权量、国家高新区、国家创新型试点城市、国家大学科技园数量位居全国前列。90% 以上的大中型企业建有研发机构，是全国创新资源最密集、创新活动最活跃、创新成果最丰硕的地区之一。

Education and Technology

Half talents are from the south of the Yangtze River. Jiangsu has always emphasized on education and nurtured generations of talented professionals. Now, Jiangsu is home to 43 academicians of Chinese Academy of Sciences, 54 academicians of Chinese Academy of Engineering, 167 colleges and universities and 1.9 million university students. The indicator for regional innovation capability ranks No.1 for eight consecutive years, and the number of patent application, patent approval, national high-tech zones, national innovation pilot cities and science parks in universities all take the top spots in China. Over 90% of medium-large enterprises have set up R&D center. All these make Jiangsu a region with the most dense innovation resources, the most innovation activities and the highest innovation productivity.

教育历史 ●————————

江苏是中国历史上状元总数最多的省份，明清时期全国 212 个文状元中，江苏出了 66 个，占全国三分之一。20 世纪初，著名实业家、教育家张謇在南通创办了全国第一所纺织学校、第一所刺绣学校、第一所戏剧学校和第一所盲哑学校。

History of Education ●————————

Jiangsu is a province with the largest number of No. One Scholars throughout Chinese history. Of the 212 No.One Scholars in the Ming and Qing Dynasty, 66 were from Jiangsu, taking up one third of the total. At the beginning of the 20th Century, Zhangjian, a famous industrialist and educationist, set up China's first textile school, first embroidery school, first drama school and the first school for the blind and the deaf in Nantong.

江南贡院是中国古代最大的科举考场
Jiangnan Gongyuan is the Largest Imperial Examination Court in China

高校教育 ●

Higher Education ●

南京大学肇始于 1902 年创建的三江师范学堂，国家首批 "211 工程"、"985 工程" 高校，有中国语言文学、天文学、化学等国家一级重点学科 8 个，医药生物技术、固体微结构物理等国家重点实验室 7 个，有两院院士 32 人，在校学生 3.3 万人。

Originated from Sanjiang Normal College built in 1902, Nanjing University is among first members of 211 Project and 985 Project with 33,000 students enrolled. It has fostered 32 academicians of Chinese Academy of Sciences and Engineering, with eight national first-class subjects including Chinese Linguistics, Astronomy and Chemical, seven national key laboratories such as Medical Biology and Solid State Microstructure.

南京大学 Nanjing University

东南大学是我国最早建立的高等学府之一，国家"985 工程"和"211 工程"重点建设的大学之一。拥有建筑学、交通运输工程、信息与通信工程等 5 个国家一级重点学科，24 个国家级、省部级重点实验室和工程研究中心。有两院院士 12 人，在校学生 3.1 万人。

As one of the earliest founded universities in China, Southeast University is one of the key univerisites included both in 985 Project and 211 Project. Having five national first-class subjects including architecture, transportation engineering, information and communication engineering, twenty-four national and provincial key laboratories and engineering research centers, it now houses twelve academicians of Chinese Academy of Sciences and Engineering and 31,000 univeristies students.

东南大学 Southeast University

南京师范大学被称为"东方最美的校园"，是国家"211 工程"重点建设的大学，拥有学前教育学、地图学与地理信息系统、动物学等国家重点学科 6 个，国家重点（培育）学科 3 个，在校学生 2.7 万人。

Having "the most bueatiful campus in the Orient", Nanjing Normal University is a key university listed in the 211 Project. It holds six national key subjects such as Pre-school Education, Cartography and Geography Information System and Zoology, three national key (fostering) subjects and 27,000 university students.

南京师范大学 Nanjing Normal University

科研力量 ●————————

江苏拥有各类独立研发机构 750
多家、专职研发人员近 75 万人。

江苏省产业技术研究院

Jiangsu Industrial Technology Research Institute

中国科学院苏州纳米技术与纳米仿生研究所

Suzhou Institute of Nano-Tech and Nano-Bionics

R&D Strength

Housing 750 independent research institutes, Jiangsu accomodates nearly 750,000 research personnel.

扬子江药业集团全景，其新型药物制剂技术实验室为国家重点实验室

Panorama of Yangtze River Pharmaceutical Group. Its Laboratory for Advanced Pharmaceutical Formulation Technology is a State-Level Laboratory.

无锡传感创新园

China Sensor Network International Innovation Park in Wuxi

超级计算机——"神威·太湖之光"在国家超级计算无锡中心研制安装，以每秒 9.3 亿亿次的浮点运算速度排名全球第一。

Sunway TaihuLight, a Supercomputer, was Designed and Assembled at Wuxi National Supercomputer Center, with a LINPACK Benchmark Rating of 93 Petaflops.

"蛟龙"号载人潜水器在江苏研制诞生，创造了下潜 7062 米的中国载人
深潜纪录，也是世界同类作业型潜水器最大下潜深度纪录。

Designed and Made in Jiangsu, Jiaolong Submersible Set a World Record of Manned Diving to 7,062 Meters.

对外开放

　　作为中国对外开放大省，江苏坚持对内开放与对外开放互动并进，131 个省级以上开发区成为对外开放的主阵地。江苏已与 226 个国家和地区建立经贸往来，结成 307 个友好城市。2016 年全省进出口总额 5100 亿美元，实际使用外资 245.4 亿美元，位居全国前列。江苏境外投资项目数量达 1003 个，数额达 130 亿美元。加大与世界各地在科技、教育、文化、人才等方面的交流与合作，江苏的影响力和美誉度持续提升。

Opening to the Outside World

As a open province in China, Jiangsu takes the dynamic approach of opening both to China and the world, with 131 provincial or above level development zones being the main platforms of opening. Jiangsu has formed trade relationships with 226 countries and regions in the world and sisterhood with 307 cities worldwide. As of 2016, imports and exports of Jiangsu stood at USD 510 billion, and Paid-in FDI hit USD 24.54 billion, with both rankings high in China.Outbound investment projects from Jiangsu hit 1,003, with an amount of USD 13 billion. As Jiangsu is intensifying exchanges and cooperation with the world in science, education, culture and HR, the influence of Jiangsu keeps rising.

开发区建设是中国改革开放进程中的江苏创造。2016年，江苏131家省级以上开发区，创造了全省一半左右的经济总量、55.2%的财政收入、82.9%的进出口总额、59.6%的固定资产投资。开发区成为全球资本、技术和人才的聚集地。

Development zones are a great achievment of Jiangsu in the course of China's reform and opening up. As of 2016, 131 provincial or above level development zones generated about half of Jiangsu's GDP, 55.2% of its fiscal revenue, 82.9% of imports and exports and 59.6% of fixed asset investment. These development zones have created a gravity field of global capital, technologies and professionals.

昆山经济技术开发区　创办于1985年
Kunshan Economic and Technological Development Zone was Founded in 1985

苏州工业园区国际科技园

International Science and Technology Park of Suzhou Industrial Park

苏州高新创业园
Suzhou Hi-Tech Innovation Park

张家港保税区
Zhang Jiagang Free Trade Zone

常州高新区
Changzhou High-Tech Zone

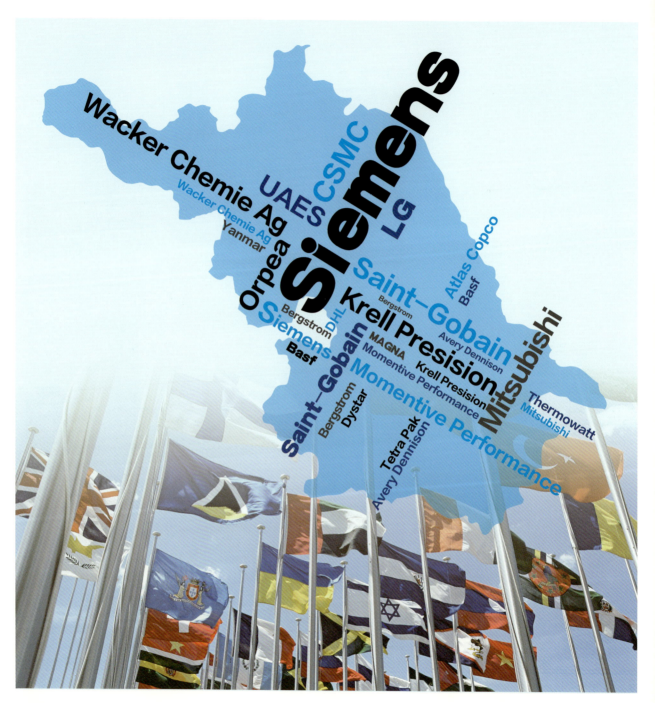

江苏着力打造高端外资集聚地，世界500强企业纷至沓来，外向型经济结构进一步优化。

As Jiangsu is gathering momentum in building a cluster of foreign capitals, top 500 companies swarm into Jiangsu, therefore further improving the outward economic structure.

博西家电发展峰会
BSH Home Appliances Development Summit

地处国家"一带一路"的交汇点，江苏主动发挥自身优势，
抢抓机遇，积极融入。

中亚班列从新亚欧大陆桥国际经济合作走廊的东方起点首发
Central Asia Cargo Train Starts from the Oriental Bridgehead of the Eurasian
Continental Bridge International Cooperation Corridor

Situated at the juncture of the Belt and Road, Jiangsu proactively leverages its advantages and grasps opportunies for entry into new markets.

由江苏红豆集团牵头投资管理的柬埔寨西哈努克港工业园
Sihanoukville Industrial Park Invested by Hongdou Group

江苏永元在埃塞俄比亚投资的东方工业园
Eastern Industrial Zone in Ethiopia Invested by Yongyuan Group

苏宁电器、徐工集团、三胞集团等一批本土优秀企业正
加速国际化进程。

三胞集团
SanPower Group

苏宁美国硅谷研究院
Suning Silicon Valley Institute

徐工巴西制造有限公司
XCMG Brazil

Top Jiangsu businesses such as Suning, XCMG and Sanpower are accelerating its pace to go global.

每年来江苏旅游的境外人士突破 300 万人。目前，在江苏学习、生活、工作的外国人已超过 10 万人。

外国人在江苏旅游
Foreigners Travelling in Jiangsu

2016 年，江苏新增涉外婚姻 1406 对
In 2016, 1,406 Jiangsu Residents Married with Foreigners

儿童作画
Children are Painting

Annual outbound tourists to Jiangsu exceed three million persons. At present, foreigners who work, live and study in Jiangsu surpass 100,000.

世界环球小姐在南京明城墙上
Miss Universe Contestants at Ming City Wall

环太湖自行车赛
Bicycle Match Around Taihu Lake

江苏发展大会

江苏发展大会由江苏省委、省政府主办，每两至三年举办一次，旨在增进与海内外江苏籍和在江苏学习、工作过的各领域知名人士的联系、交流和合作。以"约在江苏、共筑梦想"为主题的首届江苏发展大会于 2017 年 5 月 20 日在南京召开。

Jiangsu Development Summit

Sponsored by CPC Jiangsu Provincial Committee and Jiangsu Provincial People's Government, the first Jiangsu Development Summit was held in Nanjing on May 20, 2017. This event will be hosted once every two to three years for promoting exchanges and cooperation between top global professionals with ancestral homes in Jiangsu and/or have stayed in Jiangsu,.

宜居生活

　　江苏聚力创新、聚焦富民，加快推进高水平全面小康社会建设，城乡居民收入大幅提升，养老、医疗等各类社会保障全面覆盖，基本公共服务水平全国领先。林木覆盖率达到22.8%，国家生态市、生态县有45个，数量占全国三分之一。特色小镇和特色田园乡村快速发展，人居环境持续改善。全省社会和谐稳定，是全国公众安全感最高的地区之一。

Livable Home

Jiangsu is accelerating the building of a moderately prosperous society in all respects through innovation and promotion of people's well-being. Urban and rural income have improved marginally, elder-care and medi-care and other social securities were accessible to every civilians and the basic public service leads the country. Forest coverage rate in Jiangsu hit 22.8%, and the number of national eco-cities and eco-counties registers at 45, accounting for one third of the country's total. The development of towns and rural tourism areas with special features picks up speed and the living environment continues to improve. As a harmonious and stable province, Jiangsu offers people the highest degree of security.

2008 年，南京市获 "联合国人居范例奖"
The Habitat Scroll of Honor Special Citation was Awarded to Nanjing in 2008

绿色家园

全省城市绿化覆盖率达41.5%。南京、扬州、张家港、昆山获"联合国生态人居奖"。六个城市荣获"国家森林城市"称号。

Green Home

Green space take up 41.5% of urban space in Jiangsu. Nanjing, Yangzhou, Zhang Jiagang and Kunshang have won UN-Habitat Scroll Award. Six cities are entitled National Forest City.

2006年，苏州市获"联合国人居环境奖"称号
The United Nations' Habitat Scroll of Honor was Awarded to Suzhou in 2006

2016年，常州市获"国家森林城市"称号
National Forest City was Awarded to Changzhou in 2016

泰州市古银杏森林公园
The Ancient Gingko Forest Park in Taizhou

江苏拥有目前亚洲最大的沿海淤泥质滩涂，自然湿地保护面积达 90.3 万公顷，全省自然湿地保护率达 43.8%。全省共有国际重要湿地 2 处、国家重要湿地 5 处，建立各类湿地自然保护区 27 处。

Jiangsu now owns the largest area of costal mudflat, and 903,000 ha natural wetland are reserved, taking up 43.8% of all wetlands in Jiangsu. There are two world-class wetlands, five national wetlands and 27 natural reserves for wetlands.

盐城市国家级珍禽自然保护区
National Rare Bird Nature Reserve in Yancheng

盐城市九龙口湿地
九龙口的生态景观堪称一绝，九条河流从南、西、北不同方向蜿蜒而来，拥有无限绮丽的湖光水色。

Jiulongkou Wetland in Yancheng
The Ecological View in Jiulongkou is Breathtaking, with Nine Rivers from the South, West and North Converging — a Real Delight to the Eye.

宿迁市洪泽湖湿地
Hongzehu Lake Wetland in Suqian

扬州市清水潭湿地
Qingshuitan Wetland in Yangzhou

南京市银杏湖生态旅游度假区
Ginkgo Lake Eco-Tourism Area in Nanjing

特色小镇 ●

目前在全国 403 个特色小镇中，江苏有 22 个城镇入选，这些小镇各具特色、富有活力，在休闲旅游、商贸物流、现代制造、教育科技、传统文化、美丽宜居等方面独树一帜。

泰州市溱潼镇
Qintong Township, Taizhou

Featured Towns ●

Of the current 403 featured towns in China, 22 are from Jiangsu, with each presenting its own characteristics and vitality. These townships is distinctive in leisure and tourism, trade and logistics, modern manufacturing, education and science, traditional culture and ecological conservation.

无锡市拈花湾小镇
Nianhuawan Township, Wuxi

苏州市七都镇
Qidu Township, Suzhou

盐城市新丰镇
Xinfeng Township, Yancheng

田园乡村 ●

江苏推进建设生态优、村庄美、产业特、农民富、集体强、乡风好的特色田园乡村。留住"世外桃源"，延续"田园牧歌"，让江苏的新农村更具竞争力和吸引力。

南京市石塘村
Shitang Village, Nanjing

常州市牟家村
Moujia Village, Changzhou

Rural Tourism

Jiangsu is pressing ahead with developing villages with sound ecology, beautiful views, competitive economic sectors, rich famers, stong unity and good public morale. To protect the "peachland away from hustle and bustle" and pass on the lifestyle of "farming, planting and herding" will enable new villages in Jiangsu to be more competitive and attractive.

苏州市沙家浜
Shajiabang Village, Suzhou

苏州市旺山村
Wangshan Village, Suzhou

幸福生活 ●────────

江苏已实现城乡居民基本医疗保险和大病保险全覆盖。平安江苏建设成效显著，社会安全感不断提高。江苏是中国开通地铁城市最多的省份。

南京有轨电车
Nanjing Tramcar

医疗保险全覆盖
Full Coverage of Medical Insurance

Well-being

Full coverage of major disease insurance and basic medical insurance among both urban and rural residents are in place. With "Safe Jiangsu" campaign underway, the sense of safety keeps growing. Jiangsu is a province with the most cities served by underground railways.

公共文化服务设施覆盖率达 95％。在全国率先实现"省有四馆（美术馆、图书馆、博物馆、文化馆）、市有三馆（博物馆、文化馆、图书馆）、县有两馆（文化馆、图书馆）、乡有一站（综合文化站）、村有一室（文化室）"的五级公共文化设施网络体系。率先实现公共文化设施全部免费开放。

南京森林音乐会
Nanjing Forest Concert

南京图书馆
Nanjing Library

南京博物院
Nanjing Museum

Public cultural facilities cover 95% of the province. Jiangsu is pioneering a five-tier system of "public access to facilities of arts, books, museum and culture at provincial level; to museums and facilities of culture and books at municipal level; to facilities of culture and books at county level; to comprehensive cultural stations at township level and to cultural offices at village level ". Jiangs is among the first to offer free access to all public cultural facilities.

江苏大剧院
Jiangsu Grand Theatre

常州恐龙园
Dinosaur Park in Changzhou

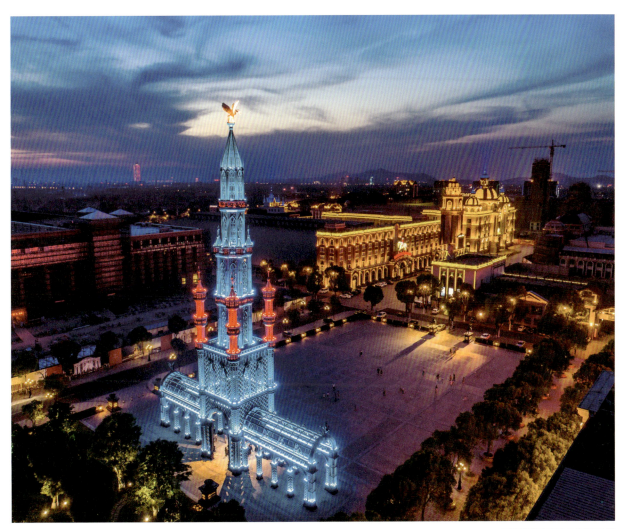

无锡海澜国际马术俱乐部
Hailan International Equestrian Club in Wuxi

南京市全景　The Panorama of Nanjing

未来，江苏将持之以恒践行创新、协调、绿色、开放、共享的发展理念，以富有时代气息的江苏精神，凝聚江苏力量，书写崭新篇章，加快推进"两聚一高"生动实践，向世界展示一个经济强、百姓富、环境美、社会文明程度高的魅力江苏。

In future, Jiangsu will unswervingly uphold the development philosophy of innovation, coordination, green development, openness and sharing. By following the Jiangsu Spirit in line with the trend of the time, it will gather strengths to open a brand new chapter of realizing moderately prosperous society at a higher level through innovation and enriching people to present to the world a charming Jiangsu with strong economy, well-off people, beautiful environment and high-degree civility.

江 苏 欢 迎 您 !

Welcome to Jiangsu !

江苏省人民政府：www.jiangsu.gov.cn

南京市人民政府：www.nanjing.gov.cn

苏州市人民政府：www.suzhou.gov.cn

无锡市人民政府：www.wuxi.gov.cn

常州市人民政府：www.changzhou.gov.cn

镇江市人民政府：www.zhenjiang.gov.cn

扬州市人民政府：www.yangzhou.gov.cn

泰州市人民政府：www.taizhou.gov.cn

南通市人民政府：www.nantong.gov.cn

盐城市人民政府：www.yancheng.gov.cn

淮安市人民政府：www.huaian.gov.cn

宿迁市人民政府：www.suqian.gov.cn

徐州市人民政府：www.xz.gov.cn

连云港市人民政府：www.lyg.gov.cn

我 苏 网

www.ourjiangsu.com

中国江苏网

www.jschina.com.cn

图书在版编目（CIP）数据

锦绣江苏 / 江苏省广播电视总台（集团）编 . -- 南京：江苏凤凰
美术出版社，2017.8
ISBN 978-7-5580-3159-5

Ⅰ . ①锦… Ⅱ . ①江… Ⅲ . ①江苏 - 概况 Ⅳ .
① K925.3

中国版本图书馆 CIP 数据核字 (2017) 第 210867 号

责任编辑　郭　渊
　　　　　曲闵民
　　　　　赵　天
　　　　　王　超
责任校对　吕猛进
英文校对　高　静
　　　　　金　旎
　　　　　舒金佳

书　　名　锦绣江苏
编　　者　江苏省广播电视总台（集团）
出版发行　凤凰出版传媒股份有限公司
　　　　　江苏凤凰美术出版社（南京市中央路 165 号　邮编：210009）
出版社网址　http://www.jsmscbs.com.cn
设计制版　江苏麦秋文化传媒有限公司
印　　制　江苏苏创信息服务中心
开　　本　889mm × 1194mm　1/12
印　　张　16
版　　次　2017 年 8 月第 1 版　2017 年 8 月第 1 次印刷
标准书号　ISBN 978-7-5580-3159-5
定　　价　198.00 元

营销部电话　025-68155677　68155679　营销部地址　南京市中央路 165 号 6 楼
江苏凤凰美术出版社图书凡出现印装错误可向承印厂调换